THE DISAPPEARANCE OF FATE

Joseph Donahue

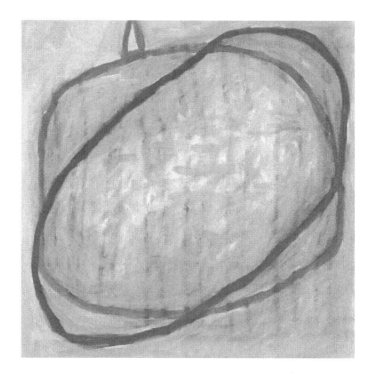

SPUYTEN DUYVIL
NEW YORK CITY

Some of these poems have appeared in *Alienocene, blackbox manifold, Brooklyn Rail, Dispatches from the Poetry Wars, Golden Handcuffs Review, Jacket2, Past Simple, PoetrySpark, Smalls, Talisman,* and *Zen Monster*.

© 2020 Joseph Donahue

ISBN 978-1-949966-50-3

cover image: Bonnie Melton *Orbit/Ellipsis*, 2014

Library of Congress Cataloging-in-Publication Data

Names: Donahue, Joseph, 1954- author.
Title: The disappearance of fate / Joseph Donahue.
Description: New York City : Spuyten Duyvil, [2019] |
Identifiers: LCCN 2019022894 | ISBN 9781949966503 (paperback)
Classification: LCC PS3554.O4673 A6 2019 | DDC 811/.54--dc23
LC record available at https://lccn.loc.gov/2019022894

for John Yau

Contents

Foam into Foam

Whenever the pen wanted to write the end,
the words led it to the beginning

Adonis

WITHOUT RENT OR SEAM

FEBRUARY

As when, gashed,
abashed, eager
to heal, at a
window
overlooking
a powder blue in-
land sea dotted with
freighters,
wind pouring
down from the
Pole on a day
otherwise
so warm the
side of a glacier
drops into the sea
and a fresh
gleam
sears the air
while, in a fable
on a stage
at a local
ecole normal,
the hero dares
a marriage
proposal
so fraught the
animals fall quiet for
the eternity of a moment —
I hear the cold
say to me:
much is
still possible

Black Die In a Clear Cup

As for me, the road will carry me
and I will carry it on my shoulder
until each thing regains its image
                                        —Darwish

A thatch, a wave, a flute song,
a struck triangle and we die, we surge,
why be afraid? Why not be like children
with a fever, resting in a yellow tent all day?
But we are not honest, have never been,
and there is nothing in the sky now
between us and a full moon other than
a dream, a storm, the Sea of Galilee
As a boy you stood on the water
Someone enfolded and protected you
(The one with doubts sinks; he cries out)
The sky is not so much teal as smoky pearl
There are deer in an icy field and foxes
whose feet are the color of the clay
or the grass in the flooded lowlands
The water is black, but it glitters
God is silent. God has never spoken
We shiver around candles in the dark
At earth's edge, black turns slate blue
Open, road of fire, on the water
We left early and traveled all night
We listen for the flicker of a spirit,
for the wind through the olive branches,
for the slender threads of sound
Night does not fall. We dip into it,
we feel it on our skin. We are not lost,
though we are in Mongolia and
the roads have closed. The waves
of snow rise to over thirty feet deep,

the tips of trees poke out of the white
We could plunge down the side of a pine
and be frozen by what never was . . .
Today you found a coin in your cake
Happy birthday, from an ancient land
where no one person can carry
a casket from the parlor to the car
The design assures it. Eight hands
are needed to grab the handles
In your grief, you will not be alone
In your grief, you will have brothers
It will be like they have come to help you
It will be like the spirit that enters us
and loses nothing of its brilliance,
like a black die in a clear cup
Like a black die in a clear cup
with a black cap on the top
The cap has a magnet in it
The black die is a hollow cube
One side is missing. So
life hides inside death. So a girl
says a magic word, flicks her wrist. So
a shake, a blur. So the black die turns white

WITHOUT RENT OR SEAM

The memoirs of
the renowned physicist
astonish the
world, reaching
even readers on sailboats
deep in the lake's
grey green
as in a forest,
leaves flickering
or still, as the wind
wills, ruffling
even the
needles of
an Arctic spruce
from
35,000
years ago
He calls earth
a heaven "without
rent or seam"

Without Rent or Seam

The water in the creek
is mostly stone

Atop a sandy spit
a scorched refrigerator

The wall facing
the street is charred

A clear sky shines blue
through the singed

hole hacked
out by firemen

ACADEMY AWARDS

Water so blue
the deep down flame
seems blue as well,
blue aura around
kindled sticks
on the ocean floor,
though a flicker of
orange is rising, now,
pulsing upward from the
bunched, burning
bundle on clean
white sand,
up through the
opaline vibrancy
A wash of heat breaks
against your skin,
whatever the depth
you're floating at,
eyes closed,
seeing what will be:
No large cities
Money obsolete
Men and women
fluttering the
implants
in their hands
to get what
they want. Yes,
a time is coming
People won't care
anymore
about Jesus,
they'll just follow
the unknown, up,

down, all around
(Until the new
Jerusalem descends
Let's just call this "remote
visualization.") Turns
out, it was a key had
drifted into my
head, but I could
only see it
from the side,
thin, a gold
and silvery light
Had I just reached out,
I could have both
had the key,
and known it!
(Dogs claw the floor,
but the cage doesn't care)
It hurts to watch the
Academy Awards,
the kisses, the backslaps,
the faces of winners
when they win,
all those hugs, the
whole room
roaring with love,
the lights swirling,
emotions high
worldwide. It is
a vision of
pure glory!
But for
days after,
I feel terrible

THE BIRTH OF STRUCTURALISM

Blood is leaving me
through the top of my head
Blood also pours across
my chest and seeps
up through my shirt
Blood is about to be
dousing my eyes. Just
as a filmy red veil
drops upwards across
my upside-down vision
a passerby pulls me out of
the pick-up that flipped
over in blowing snow
He is, it would seem,
none other than the
recently deceased
Claude Levi-Strauss
"Structuralism," he
confides, while binding
my wounds,"began
as a dream much
like the one we are
now in." In *that* dream
he found he could play
the harpsichord, but
while at the keys
he dislocated
his shoulder, and
wound up on
a morphine drip
"Take these tickets"
he says. "I have seen
Brazil so much I
no longer need to go

I close my eyes and
I'm in the wild
once again, intuiting
the shape of all thought"
Then, as if canvas
poked through
places in a painting
where all the scenes of
human life were
richly rendered,
a whirl of white
blinded me

THE HERE OF THEN, THE THEN OF THERE

My ancestors are buried in the desert
but I wake at a table, pitchers are flowing,
the scent of roasted meat drifting in . . .
So affirmed the self-others-see to the self-no-one-sees,
whose name is the turning of black to slate-blue
at the dip of the earth, and the scamper
of a flock above the road where
sea hits stone and flies into the sky
Workmen tear down a building
Ages fly by, but a kiss begun in the
9th century has not concluded
You were not there, yet I felt the heat
of your breath. I had spent harrowing nights
lost in a self that never was, travelling
towards the self that always is,
living on the anguish you sent me
But how can I praise you? All I know of
you is the pulse of my blood in the darkness
It may be, as you say, that the eternal
left a jewel on my doorstep, but
can I give thanks? An angel puts
dust on our tongues. An angel
lets us die clawing at the earth until
we awake deep within the mind
of a dervish, observing that all
sound is the song of the beloved
who brought me out of death
The water rises into the sky
where the sun is lifting, but what
does the match have to lose when
all it touches is so ready to burn?
The doctor's office, a travel agency
No one knows where they're going,
or how a dead world feels so alive

Tots scramble over wet rocks
A mother of many, a blonde in
a bathing suit, just after dawn,
crouches, amid the seethe of
breakers, cracked, on rocks, a clam
Shell bits picked out, she drinks
a raw breakfast, her curious
off-spring are informed: there is
nothing to love save for our desire
that love happen. Last night in
Tangiers I climbed a stair,
found myself in a field, at a
party for a Moroccan novelist
with a marvelous style
It was the festivity the dying
lament they miss, on the nights
between their death and their funeral
Immense affection washed me
into waking, startled though
I was to feel so honest, so ready
to admit my lies. First among them:
that I had taken ritual Japanese
baths before, but when I was done
I saw the other women had only
gotten as far as one arm. So I
washed again, very slowly
Still, when I looked around,
each of the others had only begun
scrubbing the other arm. Finally
a gnarled old peasant woman
offered to wash my hair. She
pressed and stroked my scalp
A buoyancy out of nowhere
filled me, a blessedness,
a song of impermanence
rising from the earth, heard

while crossing rushing water
in rainy darkness as a train
shakes the bridge beams
Yesterday someone said: you
don't seem to be around much
I replied: Forms pass in and out of
existence at great speed. I agree
to be in time only to the extent
I refrain from leaving it

FUTILE SERENADE

Love dispels
the hallucinations
of home: a brightly colored
bird bounces on a stripped branch
A huge mirror atop
a ridge fills with sunlight,
as does a dell below,
unlit since the
continent
took shape
Spattering light
dazzles. White gold
pools on a forest path,
the trunks of the trees
glow black
And the song
heard then, was it
Futile Serenade? Now
nothing survives discernment
aside from gossip: some
scandalous liaison,
news of which
is spreading
mouth to mouth
like a mask
hooked to a tank
of ether at a dance party
Who is not amazed?
As if the lovers had assumed
the heads of animals,
though some
find them less
than fantastic
"She looks like a

porn star, a not very
well-paid porn star"
I am unrepentant,
a mezzo in revolt against
trouser roles, who
would be a beauty
gathering cursed
blossoms for
my beloved (they
wither in my hands)
as I sing, "I, a mortal
with mere heart call
to you who are
immortal, who live
in a house where the sun
folds then sinks into a cave . . ."
The last light gathers
in a pond beneath
the glass floor
A ruin wall runs
through the bedroom
A wanderer arrives on foot
from Mongolia,
where, he tells us,
waterfalls freeze
from the inside out
He offers a traditional
Mongolian greeting:
"In whose arms
do you awaken today?"
(If only I could say your name,
praise your eyes,
lips, hair, intelligence
and beauty, if only, that is,
this were Mongolia,
a land where they

honor love)
Rain rinses the air
The dark shines
The world veers toward
days of least light, and
all passions are
clandestine,
are dreams
devoted to the
decollation of a saint,
when our words will be like
bleach spilled
on a strip of film,
the emulsion
frothing, the
image pulling
away from
the plastic

Where We Are as if We Were

Moss drying to a gold brocade
a weird dream flies through my head
as during my year in Japan when
I poured my heart out, so, to
strangers at a ritual bath
(Soak me in light, now, till
the shadows pass) At a dance
club in Osaka I heard:
"Where's your halo?" My
answer was so hilarious that
before long I was married
At first, love was like the Gulf,
tepid but refreshing as, snorkeling,
we found, in glowing sand,
the wreck of a U Boat. Then,
love was like a wild deer
eating from my hand. By the
end, love was long hours at
the Hong Kong Exchange
where none dared mention
the Cultural Revolution, how
Mao lay in bed all day, depressed
Right then I remembered the
first time I had sex. I'd dropped by
after school to play ping pong
with her son but she called
me upstairs. I think I was nine
Her breasts were hypnotic
beneath her pajama top
Upset, she told me to undress
and lie down naked, beside her
Then, naked herself, she held me
I could smell the salt where
her tears had streaked her face

The world was weeping that day
John Kennedy had just been
shot earlier that afternoon
By her grace I was spared the
national agony, though in
my research into what I call
"Pleasure Trauma," I argue
ecstasy is worse than pain
Any pleasure can wreck you
A compliment, a mild flirtation,
even just a movie where people
express joy, and your
life becomes unbearable
unless seen as a river moving
when the trees on the banks
are full of autumn leaves,
the rich grey of its flow, with
sand shining out of nowhere, and
the skeleton of a chair on a spit
The muddy mustard buckling
of water is so thick with silt
boat after boat gets stuck
Year by year, the river widens,
rises; chalk-marks appear
at the anticipated levels,
in colors too unbelievable
to be associated with the
state agency in charge. Still,
it's exhilarating to consider
what all these beloved places
will look like under water,
seen only through the billowing
run-off washing down from
some sparsely populated state
to the north, where political
prisoners call home a Bible

a blanket, and a cup. Yes,
all ideas die, but not till
some are "proven true"
Though perhaps for you
death can be just a fund set
aside for your needs, not,
certainly, to be looted
but cozened, fed, filched
from only amid the glee of
contractors who behold the
magnitude of future
renovations to the room
once home to a spectacularly
sordid happenstance, as the
younger generation might
recall, that wild party
where a suicide try by
a distraught girl won scant
sympathy, even as, lightly
bloodied, she revived, and
proclaimed: These are seasons
never experienced before,
so how can it be said
they are seasons at all?
For me, seasons are like
minutes, they don't return

Without Rent or Seam

Pain? *Gone.* Yet
you live on, amid

many in that
same pain,

or in pain much like
that. You, feeling

their feeling it,
feeling their hoping

their pain will, as
did yours, pass

away in the
night, leaving

them alive,
awake, in

bodies once
more a delight

WITHOUT RENT OR SEAM

Would this were Mercury,
deathly heat on one side,
freezing dark on the other,
a planet more honest
than earth, where
the mist before dawn
merely hides a herd of deer
by a former tuberculosis hospital
now a boarding school
atop an outcropping where
they once hung people
On Sundays, my dad,
with a vanload of state
hospital mental patients,
drove here from the city
I romped the wilds
with them, adored the
black and white dairy
cows in a green dell
I will remember that
happiness forever,
even in my grave of
canal water, black, shining
much as since the days of
the paddy camps,
when glory shone from
the faces of our ditch-
digging ancestors

WITHOUT RENT OR SEAM

A night

doubly dark —

trees

blotting out

moon and stars,

and the

ambulance,

quiet, lights

shooting past the

driveway of

the man who

collapsed,

(the stroke victim

next door

about to die,)

and pulling

into the

wrong

one, mine

WITHOUT RENT OR SEAM

If, before sending
it, John Cage tore the
package, is the tear
a part of what he has
sent? A part of the gift?
Is it, in fact, the truer
gift, all inside the
package merely
the means for the
tear to be sent? Was
the tear meant to show
the bounty of the
given, the glitter, say,
of what's wrapped
around what's
within? Or do
the depths just
highlight the hole,
the rip, the gouge,
the gentle death-blow
visited upon the
otherwise properly
sealed parcel,
the seal itself
not yet torn?

NIGHTS IN TUNISIA

Evenings, they all
took turns, greeting
me with such lovely
dinner dishes,
brought right
to the door, that
whole season of
goodbye to all
those items
she had
saved for me

Nights, we drank
in a tavern till four
It was wonderful,
hearing about
sailors, and
singing ballads
about the sea

One night, I
forgot a song
I once knew well
It bothered me

Finally, I gave
up and went back
to my mother's
huge, unhappy
house, to all
the tenderly
boxed nothings
I had no place
for, back home

Then at dawn
the phone rang!
One of my new-
found friends
from the tavern
recalled the song!
He sang it to
me as the
sun came up

OTHERS, IN DISBELIEF

Others around,
in disbelief
at the clear flow of
feeling, between the two,
so, inappropriate,
so close to
scandalous,
right there, in
the midst of
the party,
in the shadow of
the porch door
near where
the bar
shone, aglow
with bottles, an
almost kiss
Then Fate
said, no,
not now
Then each
drifted back
to lesser
loves

Manhattan Shadows

It's Heaven's light on
a leafless tree hung with
fright masks where a snake climbs
It's a streak of yellow across a black pool,
a first glow on the grass along the empty road,
in a misty field, by a fuel tank
that fell off a space ship,
dropped, like the chandelier
last night, and shattered
It's a wedding on New Year's Eve
Guests in a line blow soap bubbles
The couple leaves the church
The soapy globes wobble
The moon is cut in half

                    *

It's an opera where
a higher consciousness
lays its claim. *There is no place I go*
where you are not. My parents would take us
We were very small. We fell asleep
A half-moon floats like crushed gift paper
and loose ribbon in the blackness
Who were the boy and the girl
once the kiss came to be?
Now age makes me an ogre,
a folded face with a failed inner life
(This movie is called *Embodiment*
All are in it.) Tremble, traveler
A hut shines in the flowers
Until this mountain peril our lives
had been exciting, but thin,
like a novel read on a treadmill

A rabbit shakes the wan grass
Why not play Christmas carols?
Instead: *A Whiter Shade of Pale*
Instead: Verdi's *Requiem*

*

Next day, the sun's just a gold hole
with a strip of cloud across it
Many believe much once thought has to be
rethought. And the words
with which thought will be
rethought, must they be alive?
Or would it be better if they were dead,
now that the abyss tips upward
and the heights are pouring down?
A stream rises, flooding the woods
You knew me, even as I was
knit in the womb. A surprise,
a presence, a last back and forth
like in a job interview: *How long*
does it take you to dress
in the morning? Depends
Would this be a hair-washing day?
An entire city turns to mud
the waves simply dissolve it
Bodies like floating deck chairs
It's like living on a hill in a city of hills
It's like living in San Francisco,
where I once made a dragon
from recycled Styrofoam
Later, in China, I was told
to devise my own re-education
I had muttered far too loudly
how Manichean Mongols
had skewed Buddhism

A simulation of my breath
blows a kite over the trees
Why escapes me: Why, that is,
we choose the slavery of this life
The manual says simply, if the part
is faulty, the screen will go blank

*

From here in space,
the island of Manhattan
looks much like the floor plan
of a Mayan temple complex,
but no altars, no buildings,
no plaza, no roads, no plants,
no Mayans, not any hint
of life, no animal or plant,
only stones, only Manhattan,
in a dream, like a close-up
of the moon. It's the
grainy dispersion
of rocks far below,
shadows of what will be:
buildings, parks, streets,
the city of your exile, that
you love, not there, but there,
in the scatter of stones,
in the cast of gravel

CORPSE FLOWER

Your spiritual life, by
contrast, were it a plant,
would not be native to some
rain forest, but to an immense desert,
fiercely inhospitable, crossed
only by satellites on their way
to some spot on the planet
worth monitoring, not
this scorched corner of it all
where blossoms spare
and intricate thrive on only a hint
of wet, a puff of molecules before dawn,
a ghost of dew too thin to glisten
What divine eye passing overhead
finds you on the way to the opening night
of an unhappy production where
some will drop their lines,
some their swords. Others will
crouch backstage, weeping,
or rush into the shattered scene
that now resembles the last chapter
of a physics textbook where
certain laws of nature
no longer align with
common sense. Suddenly
it seems, the Stone Age awakes
It has become the Bronze Age
Arrowheads of flint are obsolete
A new tribe floats in from the east
with different linguistic origins
and new ideas about how
to dispose of the dead
Party lights dangle across
a deserted construction site

Early evening. The pale houses
seem steeped in ink. The river
could only be the Hudson
The shreds of water lift your heart,
which is not untroubled, as the enclosed
but unfurnished room darkens
and is torn into shadows
The last light of day glitters
minutes more in the flowing
Lightning pierces the earth
Now the earth can be fruitful
as before, in the shadow
of Aeria, city of air, said to be
magnificent, though only
these clouds have survived
It pains me. That was my city
My home is drifting from me
My home has blown away
My home now is at most
fireworks, green, orange,
white, blue over a lake
announcing how the divine
flies free of its attributes,
leaving the world adrift in ash
Though many years later
you waved me over
In the huge lecture hall
you had saved me a seat
The professor spoke clearly
but I couldn't follow him
You were too close
My heartbeat was
all I could hear

THE VOW

So the mantra modulates
from die, die, die, to paradise is now
The sun is overhead, as in an illustration
from a language acquisition manual
for students in distressed places
with erratically maintained
social services, where a regime
can begin and end on the same day
Puget Sound reappears on the left
Wash of warmth over face and arms,
then a touch of a chill damp air
Our bodies are planets that do not
rotate as they loop their star
They face the light in adoration
while freezing in the dark
Our bodies are like a mosque
that is also a cathedral. So it would
seem, just back from southern Spain,
from beaches in the morning, naps
after lunch, then out on the cool streets
in the evening, when the darkness
caused by our deeds lightens
and we listen to courtship tales
from the faculty of a local high school
The French teacher is captivating
Bright blue eyes, play of black hair
She was tired of gloomy French
men who were "intellectuals"
So she put on silver pants,
orange shoes, came to America,
to Disneyland, in fact, and met a man
who knew no French. But his face
was so open and welcoming . . .
All are changed by the tale they tell,

even the bitchy one, who decreed
he would test his lover, and was
a total asshole for ten years
They all knew about the vow,
lived through the era of bitchiness
Right at ten years, he stopped,
became kind and loving

The Forest of Water

femme fatale

A beach, a bonfire, a girl in cut-offs. Slung from her shoulder, a toy gun. She's fifteen, sixteen, wild brown hair, pulled back, pale skin, freckles, dark lashes, large dark eyes, almost without coronas, as if always dilated, as if pure pupil or secretly high, all the time. She's evasive, abrasive, flirtatious, her pale blue long-sleeve clingy shirt cut low above her breasts. On the shirt, small cornflower blossoms. A shirt to be slept in. She looks like she woke up, wandered out. Night again. The boys at the bonfire crave what's under that shirt. But the girl has that gun, that plastic Thompson gun. Not afraid to use it. The barrel sparks. The girl puts her weight on one leg, a beer held back from view. (This is, what, thirty-five years ago?) She's moody, witty, abrupt, talking to a boy, then suddenly, *Da. Da da da. Da.* Pointing, pulling. Syllables and sparks: *Yuh dead*, she exults. In her voice, utterly entrancing: a hint of New York street tough.

at the edge of the forest of water

Love called these children, culled them, from Rhode Island, Massachusetts, New Hampshire, New York. Love cared deeply. He gave them the ocean with islands on the horizon and a wide stretch of sand on which to talk and frolic and fall silent. Gave them pot, beer, Quaaludes, uppers, hashish, rum. And, birth control. Gave them the kiss, and all that leads up to it: the talk, the standing close, the flash of eye, touch of sunburn and salt water. Our skin was too much for us. We were burning inside it, even on cool nights, even in the whisper and exhalation of waves.

the glance

Along the road at night, steps on gravel, you're walking one
way, she the other, not the femme fatale, another, home from her
summer job at the corner store cash register, pink shirt, white jeans,
light of a passing car behind you, the light washes over her, she's in the
dark again, she looks at you, she says hi to you. Who were you before
that, before a fourteen-year-old girl said hello? It starts now, the story
that shapes all your thought: a beautiful smart girl just off work walks
home on a road at night.

hidden

An old travel kit, full of letters, letters full of days, events in
the days, all time in a schoolgirl hand, and you, full of feelings, now,
from those days, paragraphs, some in third year French, floating into
you. Her tales of tears, her plaintive meditations, her droll tableaux of
the mundane, her delirious hints, her earnest wonderings, her pages
dashed off moments after parting, so direct, so thoughtful, so sharp,
her sentences, some on the back of a torn menu, are, for you, now, the
only true stylistic perfection.

the couch

Kissing at night, as summer burned down, kissing every night,
drunken kissing, stoned kissing, unassisted kissing, after the furtive
hand holding, warm sweep through the limbs, beneath sunburned,
ocean-dipped skin, words and, greater, silences. There was, must have
been, at some point, a first night on which the hand was held, the
first of an anything but casual closeness, the brush of the fingers of
one against the inside of the hand of the other, the fingers slip and
mingle, the longest millisecond of all time, the wait for a response,
tender or impetuous, or slow building pressure, and soon, kissing,
long intervals of kissing, right there, lying on the couch together,

all others, overhead and asleep, the couch by the huge window, the ocean right there, sand and water and the kissing, waves breaking, the pull of stones back towards the sea, white sand, moonlight on white sand as the kissing kept going on, almost wearying, certain moments, but then renewed, intensified, some preliminary wandering strokes, nothing like what would be, once the course of the kissing deepened, the mind might wander far, the continuous sun-storm of the kissing, as if bodies were ports one ventured out from, and came back to, and set forth again, and night was nothing more than what aids and protects the kissing, walls of moonlight, whirls of water, so banal all day, so magical at night, the couch where the kissing occurred, slender bodies clutch, twist, lie in stillness, as if they were only adumbrations of the water, as if at night they became, while the kissing continued, creatures of water, witness now borne by the sweat of their bodies, they are bones and water and warmth, one lying atop the other, holding the face of the other, or side by side, tormenting each other, with touching, and then the kissing would resume.

passing stranger

Long pants, dress shirt, no tie, dress shoes in one hand, a six-pack in the other, the man with the nervous tic is crossing the powder blue sheets of sheen on the flat, dark, low tide evening sand. The tic was this: his head snapped to one side. Whatever else he might want to see, the curve of the coast, sunset colors on the wet sand, the waves, the cape, the islands, freighters or sails, the dazzle of all he walked in, he kept looking at them, he kept looking away from them.

femme fatale

As on the night spent kissing the girl with the gun, the dangerous girl, brazenly and late, in the front yard, beer or wine or pot swirling through the interplanetary spaces inside your brain. You had contrived to walk her home, the dew already gathering on the chill grass, her eyes deep and black, to which, later, you would ascribe the most complex interiority, but now you were pressed together, under stars, in earshot of the sea, she's murmuring sarcastic, devastating enthrallments, she's so soft, fleshy even in her thinness, things are being said, then kisses, her gun slung across her back.

homage to Kawabata

Those waking hours not lost thinking about a girl or kissing a girl were lost in reading. Whole moments at a time you crossed into the world of the novelist who entranced you. In August heat, you were not in New Hampshire, at the shore. You were in Japan, in the snow country. You saw the house of love burn. You felt the cold stars pour through you.

glitter

And one time walking back from the rocks, that jagged outcropping under the sharp curve in the coastal road where the boy and the girl would steal off with a wineskin full of wine, and laugh and guzzle in the wash and snap of the waves breaking and rushing into the channels of stone, holding hands, knee deep, mid-tide curl of water, legs streaming the gleam of the algae, feathering swirls of light trailing their steps. They might kiss, a bit, before returning to the boardwalk. Delighted, giddy, how stoned they were, their young hands stroking the skin of the ocean, watching their touch turn to white fire.

masque

Love so spun our heads with assurance that we would be cherished, known, fathomed, touched, forgiven, that we enacted a Renaissance masque without ever knowing it. Who can really say who it is they kiss or curse, who it is they confide in, who it is betrays them, who it is writes love letters in the off season, who it is keeps love letters in a box for thirty years, who it is dreams all is again. At this point in the play, nothing has happened yet. Pure ideas are personages, your love among them. You have only just now been introduced.

the creek

Some nights the boy and girl sat by a creek in the dark. It was almost an inlet, almost a cove, almost a path, almost the edge of a dark and fabulous forest suddenly rising above the reeds in the darkness. But on other nights, on the other side of the coast road, the salt marsh reeked with rot, with an almost frightening funk. Those nights, the creek warned them: go away. Flee. Come back in fifty years, if you choose to come back at all.

love letter

This was the moment for the writing of the ultimate letter, to the one if not to the other. And so, to bear across days and weather and distance the truth about to be entrusted to paper, what seemed to you your neediest plea, a guide was required, to lead you into the heart of the femme fatale, from your cell deep in the boarding school autumn, an until recently unheard of hallucinogen. Her letter lay open before you: her vibrant pages, her eerie ink drawings, moons in the margins, bare trees and birds, it's tone by turns teasing and abject, a taunt to the entirety of your feelings. Her orange-gold stationary glowed. But what, really, in the counsel of those unprecedented chemicals, did you write in return? Did you even manage a salutation? Did you even come close to writing your ultimate letter, your pen wavering at the plunge of the M, at the uptake of the ells, the ink outrunning the script, the rolls, loops, counter spins of what would conclude your greeting, not to mention the meadows of confession that would await you after the peaks of her name?

the couch

Between not yet kissing and never again kissing, night after
night, that one summer, the boy and the girl side by side, looking,
steady gaze, into each other's faces, a sometimes ticklish scamper of
lips down the neck to the shoulder, up the neck into the ear, in the
living room dark, almost laughing, the aged, upstairs, abed, a pause,
then fresh intensities, lips pressed to the point of pain, till each could
sense the skull of the other, the skull of wonder. Tongues linger,
taunt, in the faint light from the ocean, from the moon on the ocean,
filling the window, hands setting forth down the back, under the shirt,
skimming the belts, slipping within. The kissing went on, kiss after
kiss, the boy and girl, side by side, waves passing through them, the
sound of surf, the ocean so close, their slight awareness of it, on the
couch, as the kissing and the touching flowed on.

the couch

Night. Day. Night. Earth turns. Kissing recurs. Bodies lean
towards lips, pressing, relenting, scraping when dry, sliding when wet,
eyes wide in slight light, and the hands, tugging, slipping, cupping,
splaying, sculpting, running through the repertoire of touch. What
could the telos of tenderness be, of the swirl of hair, of the divinatory
scratch, the rake of nails, but to call up an ecstasy on the horizon, a
never before sun, a perfect earth, about to be, a *paradiso* of fingertips,
the stroking feather-light tracing of what might be a new, celestial
alphabet. At the edge of the sea the kissing goes on. The room glows,
moonlight spilling, over the water, over their bodies, bodies just so
much salt and water. The ocean orders them to kiss, to keep kissing, to
say only simple things like, that was incredible, or, you can touch me
there, it's really ok, before waves shush them, boy, girl, in the dark, on
a couch, the two on their way so what if neither knows where, here at
the rim of the sea, at the edge of the forest of water, or suspects what
else the dark rends as it renders. These moments are a marvel, are a
couch in a house by the ocean, at night.

bonfire

On the beach at night, all around a bonfire bursting with plastic baggies of gasoline, slashes of light and shadow falling on all. A beer can in one hand, held down, hand on the top, fingers covering the gleam of the top of the can, if a parent drifted by, came down from the party up on the deck, Thompson gun in the other hand, thin legs frayed with cutoff threads, exuberant, caustic, saucy, impenitent, virtually murderous, the femme fatale, merrily passing the barrel across the chests of all the boys there, deciding who would die.

femme fatale

They loved the Velvet Underground. They loved the song, *Femme Fatale*. They loved, some of them, the Dietrich film behind the song, *The Blue Angel*. Song and movie doubled the pull of the dangerous girl, of her plastic gun, the moody girl, pale skin, large eyes, and dark lashes, her moodiness often tipping toward havoc, a glance down, away, lingering, deflecting the perpetual attention, bouncing that bolt into the ground, that lightning strike, darkness at midday, in full sunlight, on the porch, out of the sea breeze, without a word. Heaven confirmed it: this girl was unhappy, unhappy, and attractive, unhappy, and attractive, and angry. What she knew about life seemed large, there, just on the other side of her silence. Boy or girl, each entered the forest of that mood, called by that face looking away from daylight, as if it were quite possible to both be a pre-Raphaelite ingénue, and to wave a toy machine gun, grabbed in a flash from her day pack. She was another Patty Hearst, albeit brunette, about to walk into a bank and be famous forever for her state of mind. She was sharply funny. No one could figure her out.

femme fatale

When she fled into the night, the night seemed enhanced, luminous in its magnitude, because she was upset, and because she stepped out into it, because her pale limbs moved through it, whether she had slipped out unnoticed, or allowed her mood to stir up a scene. No one else left the way she left. There was little understood of the night, of the ritual of gone into the night, apart from what it revealed of you, of your moods, which touched them all, boys and girls alike, and the waves, and the planets, and the stars.

homage to Kawabata

Pages unfolding so slowly, they seemed to enter the body through the fingertips, through the touch of the fingertips turning the pages, the pages of images, of wonders that drift up through nerves and blood into the mind, as, now and then, as if out of nowhere, disgust intensified the beauty. As if out of nowhere, as if into the mind forever, an observation such as: "He spent much of his time studying the death agonies of insects."

skim boarding

A thin low-tide sheet of water on the rich flat sand. A sparkling swirl, a gleam. In the distance, the tapering, tumbling, water. High tide idles off shore. A plywood circle tossed while running with a light spin slaps the long ripple of seawater. The runner hears the slap, the runner decides the slap sounds right. The runner while running factors in the angle of the board, stretches out his or her stride, then, with a light jump, steps onto spinning board, crouches, skids across the top of the water, for several seconds slightly flying.

dream

     Wherever I was living, I opened the door. You were there, as beautiful as when you were a girl. You were glad to see me. It was quite a shock: that you were there, that you looked so much like I remembered you, and that you were in a wheelchair. We chatted. You put your hands, palms down, on your thighs, and said: I don't feel anything, here, anymore. Then: more catching up. Then, you moved your hands to your lap, pressed your fingers between your thighs, and said: I don't feel anything here either. The apartment hallway was quiet and empty. It was such a miracle to see you. It was clear: we both were overjoyed. I knelt beside the chair. I hugged you. I felt your tears on my neck. They slipped under my collar. They sank onto my chest. I felt the catch of your breath within the broken ring of my arms.

Eros

     Eros called them onto a stage of sand and rocks, had them act out their transformations, so that their hearts, souls and bodies might be mingled in the glass bowl of the air, be heated and cooled, be the primordial salt compounded into all parts of what they were to be. Eros, you gave us bodies, then made us ghosts. Decades later, I see teenagers at a bus stop, flirting and sulking. I see what is happening to them. I want to cry out.

homage to Kawabata

     And around that long-ago time, it was in the papers: at the age of seventy-three, Kawabata committed suicide, whose sole artistic aim had been, he once said, "to beautify death."

dream

Last night she alighted in his sleeping mind, as beautiful as when they were teenagers, but she was older, a woman, in a loose fitting summer dress. She stood where the houses once were, and were again. Another structure was there, all glass and white beams, the size of a single room. The time of day in the dream was nighttime. This room seemed to glow. White curtains flickered inside it. There was a bed, covers pulled down at one corner. They looked at the room, a mesmerizing cube that seemed to be floating over the moonlit shallows. She said: So much that hurt us now makes no difference. Let's lie down on that bed. It will be better even than sex was. Stay with me. We can look out at the ocean and talk.

In an Orchard at Night

In an Orchard at Night I

During the time that they are veiled, they observe
sudden glimmerings that take them by surprise
                                        —Qushayri

The earth had never
been more than a cloud

     *

And by a dry streambed
below a gold hill,

such states of being
as a drunk, or

an ascetic,
feels,

would
feel

     *

Another night, why did the
light mean more

than the
shadows?

     *

(A possible answer: So that
this could be the book

of
flashes)

*

Another night, you, too, had risen
to where these ephemeral

happenings are
continuous

*

(Or, having stayed put, just
stayed as you were, you let your

heart become
a shroud)

*

A young man in a blue coat just went out your door
stepping over a pile of your

bottles, books, and
unopened bills

*

(Isn't he, in some
presumably ongoing
life, your son?)

*

Back and forth, too quick to fathom:
the salamander

dazzles the
dog

*

Another night, the canal water was
so black it could hardly

mirror the
flames of the

floating bowls of
burning oil

*

(The flames seem to lie
on the water

for a moment,
then sink)

*

Another night, —
thunder so monumental you

could not miss it, or
the blinding

blank
breaking

across
her sleep,

across, enfolding,
a dress, on a hanger,

hung from the top of a door
The dry-cleaner

plastic
trembled

*

Another night, over the black
wash of the trees

a full moon
smeared low,

hazy, the tasty
shade

of an
apricot

*

Another night, round midnight,
a helicopter swept low,

descending
to the hospital

*

Another night: To the abiding presence of
what else were we

so blind on
any day?

＊

The decree of a
dream so

utterly
forgotten is:

No detail shall ever be
swept back to

the alien domain
of waking

＊

(As when, in the midst of a
Moravian Love Feast,

the color of the
ribbon on

our bonnets announced
to all whether or

not we would

entertain

a suitor)

*

Another night, the poetic image is a portal,
a friend said. Look through it

What do you see
on the other side?

Are there trees?
What is the sky like?

Do the people have faces,
or are they all wearing masks?

*

Grass so dry, its turning white
At dawn, the yard looks like an astonishing frost

*

Another night, a dream,
a clay statue, handed to you,

a whirling
inside it, you

can feel it pass, pour
deep into in your hands,

into the bones of
your hand, as if your daughter

allowed you, with
this gift,

to feel, at last,
some first force, to marvel

at the depth of the red, in the clay, the flicker
of orange and red

within it, as if
drawn into the shaping of it

from the ridges and
ravines all

around, and sunk
within the clay,

now
and then,

a wave, a rift,
a shadow

*

A tree, a branch, a blossom, a sliver of
bluish red that has

darkened, but
all the

light in the sky
still bends towards it

*

Another night, a river dropped into a desert
Hundreds of miles away, the

wells in the village
began filling

*

Another night, a woman, in a blue-green
chemise the shade

distance itself
would

shine with
in a Japanese print,

was saying: I emerged from a gold mine
deep below the water table

We rode down
harrowing

passages in utter blackness knowing
the walls had once been

coral reefs, and that
the chief

cause of death in this mine
is drowning

The sides of the
shuttle train scraped the walls

The driver had the
only light

Now and then we passed
a lone miner, deep into his own tunnel, flat out, with

a lamp, in
mud, clawing,

mud as black as a
black snake on a black road,

though at night
moonlight

tends to make
its skin

glisten
as it glides

        *

Another night, night after the
night of

the costume party: crepe, streamers, wands,
masks on the floor,

silver, glittering
confetti,

all were still there, the room
so empty, as if, later that

evening, in
the mist of the

fun, all those
there were swept off

the
planet

*

A book like a boat
like a bird like a book

like a caulked box
to float away in,

looking up, in a depth of
pure inundation, at the stars

*

Last night, at last,
        the last night

*

                (The sky overhead, at once
                emerald and purple

                and a glowing
                black, as if

                there were gold
                beneath the black,

                as if to look
                up, into it all, at

                this exact moment
                placed you, as the

philosopher
might say,

"in the totality of the
sphere of one's heaven")

*

No one there yet, to think your thoughts
No one there, in the not yet nowhere of your head

*

No one there yet, with marvelous truths to tell you,
as over a pillow, in the dark, upon waking

*

Pins, screws, segmented strips

Blood-threaded

grooves of
titanium

gleam

*

(Mending done
Metal parts on a metal tray)

*

Another night, collarbone, ribs, pelvis
form a Z inside you

To see the Z, step back
Watch yourself

shambling on
in warm sunlight

      *

Your bones propose a letter

cutting from your upper left shoulder
across your chest then down,

striking across then diagonal
down your torso,

through lungs, heart,

through whatever else,

as would be legible
to some leapt from shadows

Spanish death
slicing you wide,

some ultimate

Zorro

      *

The last night, the end,
the consummate

zed,

that last sound
    after which all
        sound
            is done

                    *

                ("This is not the jewelry I like

                Can you take it back?

                Try to give me what goes
                unnoticed by most,

                a minimalist
                tribute,

                a trinket

                barely making
                visible

                the light

                around me")

            *

Another night, within which we were just the

non-existent

objects

of

God's

knowledge

    *

Then our hearts began beating

    *

A lake so dry the lakebed has been looted

    *

Soaked trees blacken, the few
leaves left,
            shine

    *

Another night, a woman in a nightgown leaning

close to her sleeping
husband's ear,

whispered, between

lightning
strikes:

I am

otherwise
loved

*

(As for you, the divine has only lightly

brushed your mind

Your world is wet, yet

you have no memory of

the downpour)

*

Another night, my tears are not for the black hole

at the heart of the Milky Way,

not for the upcoming flare-out of the sun,

but for the moon, pulling away,

each orbit, toward

some new and unlit

life in the night

*

And when at noon
water shone

without shadows
in the hell of a well,

       I knew this to be
          Egypt

     *

A roadside rock-pile
        in relentless heat

     *

A glare where, with
a breeze, onto the dust,

the deep shade
of a mul-

berry tree
      cascaded

     *

         *at a memorial**

Months after the memorial,

it will turn up,

mid a stack
of CDs,

her stick-it note
still radiating generosity

from a loan

Lichtbogen

*

("— Will
we hear,

in her music, in this
sad tribute,

tomorrow,
what went on

in her mind, what
thoughts she had when

alone and
listening?"

" — No,
they, too,

are dead. But, arising
from dots of

ink as
sound,

thought itself
will be reborn")

*

("— Is it true,
a word once

set the universe
before us, to be seen,

to be grasped in its totality,
a word so exact, so right,

that the universe
appeared

much as we had
secretly imagined it

and we rejoiced, confirmed
in our most sublime

intuition?"

"—Yes, though it

troubles me
that

I forget
that word")

                    *

Upside down in the storm outside
                    leaves twisting in the wind

                    *

A man lifts the lid
of a grand piano

He chants nonsense of
pure grief into the hollow

Slowly during
his wails and cries

the audience
understands that

what they are hearing,
in the rafters of the dome

floating down
with the sound of rain is

the echo of the
vibrating strings

               *

The piano having been,
          in life, your instrument

               Awakened by the grieving
                    vocalist the un-struck notes

                    long for the fingers that
               no longer touch them

          *

Another night, in Thailand, whirls of fireflies
around a tree, gradually
syncing

their flashes,
these winged

nerve-endings

dazzled the darkness

*

Another night, will the rehearsal last all night, or will

the soul finally fly

to Alexandria,

Constantinople,

Tehran,

and lay a rose at dusk

on a grave beside

a mosque?

*

The canal, pink and orange

A librarian in Lowell is walking
to the evening shift

the public library

open to eleven because
the citizens, there, crave that

the unknown
    light the night

    *

Pale copper leaves

    A house goes black

A shawl of light
in a window,
a wispy face

    *

    (That may be all
    my mother is now, an

    aghast gaze)

    *

In the failing twilight
    the road-crew
        kicks a soccer ball

    *

Many of the other exiles
in Saint Petersburg, or Athens

or L.A., recall that

infamous secular paradise,

all smiles, music, sex

Gypsy boats in bull rushes

Legendary drums

—all talk was French—

as, just recently, at an
outdoor fête in
Santa Fe

*

Such a paradise as was just outside the capitol

in the 1940s

Blue tiles in snow

Architecture magnificently abstract

*

When summer came,

we would sip beer, smoke
opium, and dip

our feet in the

Euphrates

*

Another night, writhing in pain
I moved through the air, out over water

The sky darkened

I dropped into the reeds and
peeled off the jacket that
gave me flight

        *

        (Will I ever know what form I had
        before I awoke, the storm
        exploding around me?)

        *

Another night, two friends are at odds
One tells the truth all the time,
the other never saw
a lie he didn't like
I love them both, and
find, with them,
I am free to be quiet,
and dream of
a perfect tree,
human forms laying
all around it, touched by
agony, wound
in cloth, some
still alive

        *

        dream

Another night, in the fountain around which guests
at a garden party made merry

were three pebbles that
needed to be saved. These
were understood to be,
though for what reason
the dream withholds,
"Jerusalem stones"
Each was to be snatched
from the devil in that water,
plucked from the onyx font,
and flung far into the
shadowy woods,
far from the lit-from-
within black stone oblong
trough, where water
coils and leaps

        *

"The fissures in the cliff
are beautiful. How

grateful, we are,
these days,

that
the earth

once rolled
in molten waves . . ."

So write the newly wed
        on a tour of the world

        *

So the cycles
of time

continued to overlap,
(should this book be believed)

Some cycles were known
intimately,

others, a lifetime
offered only a glimpse of

(Should this book be believed, with
all its glimmerings, risings,

flashes, pangs, and
onslaughts)

When they
conclude,

we will still be
(should this book be believed)

*

Let all
fall through

all, was the thought
Or, all will fall

through all,
where I lie

Or, where
thought lies,

all falls, let that
be what is

Let lies fail
and fall,

let thought
be what

is, be
all

IN AN ORCHARD AT NIGHT   II

The light of the sun
reaches through your

closed eyes. The
day exists to wake

only you. Only you, and not
whoever died in your

place, yesterday,
and dropped

into the
dirt today

*

Or is your sleep
not yet deep enough,
not yet as deep

as the lilac,
its drops of

dried blood,
its crease

in the white petals,

its yellow
center only
the sun touches

*

Lord, heal me,

my bones are vexed

*

As are the pins, plates,

the titanium screws

which some far-off future

crematory

will no doubt sizzle

into brilliant

commemorative

spatters

*

Each night on this

ward called "The Orchard"

   dips me in embalming fluid

*

I who once lived atop a tower

floating on the ocean

I tipped back, dropped,

pink streaks, falling sun,

warmth of a pale

blue depth and

dazzling coral reefs,

fish in their quick,

cloudy spasms

                    *

My long ago first love should be

bandaged, in

a hospital herself,

but she's nonplussed,

slipping into

a shimmering

blouse,

heading to work,

huge welts

running black

and blue down the left

side of her

torso

        *

            (It's not clear if she

            has a left

            breast

            anymore)

        *

But then, few in a single lifetime see past

the shimmer on the purple

of the robes in the

shunga print

        *

Commission me

to raise
                a grotto from the wreck
of a tennis court, to

summon a trellis
so complex

it will never,

in our

lifetimes,

teem with vines

    *

        (Glorious night, lives done!

        Some such garden

        Some such

        bodies)

    *

That derelict season

between death and rebirth

that must be

  what drops away

    below the staircase

beyond the door
soon to be
    stepped

through into stretches of
    white and yellow and rose

the door,
which is still only
half-open, and beyond,

a depth of dark

*

The sheets of flame
hang like a French tapestry
in the oak-walled library of a childhood home

*

A distraction from the
            suicide note left
                        on your pillow

*

The curtain slipped back
blood was all across the lower bunk bed

The 9-1-1 operator advised:
"Feel for a pulse"

*

The stillness, then,
filled your fingertips

It touches whatever
you touch, now

It's a part of
every pleasure

*

Then a night with the effect of lightning

on photosynthesis

*

        (Were these leaves any
        more pale, they would be
        apple petals)

*

Another night, fluctuations in
the moons of Jupiter: Europa and Io

One is volcanic, lurid,
The other, all fractured ice,

"exquisite, like a flawed pearl"

*

Another night, all was Antarctica in twilight

where, with a squad of
photographers,
we shot rocks and
water and ice

twenty hours a day

as a continent
flared open

*

The first

bird

is hesitant

as if

the thought of

light

were now to be

the call to
song

and not

rising fire
and

a new

horizon

*

Much as a suspended chord is

one not found yet, one

awaiting whatever

instrument

*

An iron frill with a hole

and a light switch

that looks like

a blue salamander

on a stone wall

*

There is depth to these
pleasures

the fact
   that is felt

      that the

fact
is felt

*

The sun is
bright and hot, but
in the shade, it's raining

*

Another night, the altar had swung wide
A staircase had appeared

*

Children ignite gunpowder in a field
The goats learn to ignore them

*

Another night, my new ID photo was nothing
but an outline of
someone seen once,
through a
window, who was
standing inside a rust-orange
building, cell phone
in hand

*

In the exact place I will die
a party is peaking

A cruise boat

Someone's older sister
is getting married on the deck

Balloons, music

Mountains ring the shimmering waters

In an Orchard at Night III

Another night, amid

orange petals

a flutter, black, alights, holds, goes

Or as in *The Iliad*, when

a warrior, killed off

earlier,

inexplicably

comes back

       *

Another night, the waiter wanted so much to be

a woman, casting spells of

femininity

makeup, elegant,

his bracelets

beautiful

       *

Another night, a man and a girl
stood at a worktable

The girl nodded, but the man, her father, was slow witted

In this old tire place
turned makeshift theater

He seemed to think another dictionary
hid inside the one

he was buzz-cutting in half

     *

         (You, too, could be said to seem

         to think that each

         thought

         presupposes

         a totality)

     *

No one can stop what is
flowing through you, at least

for this snip of each day,

in Ramallah, or Paris,

hour free of your cell, the
cell turns to sweet white fire

     *

And then morning, in a café
in Aleppo

sipping coffee,
while the apocalypse

happens, just down the street

      *

Lacking sunlight, the green intensifies

        A glowing grey soaks the hospital corridors of the sky

      *

And then morning, a bomb-scare
clears a public building

People mill in the street, sip tea,
wait to see the fabulous police dogs

      *

Another night, rats gnaw the scroll

They eat away at the Pentateuch
until there is nothing left

They are the eleventh plague
They destroy the record of the first ten

So that in such a winter
rat scat is holy

Rat scat records

the name of the Lord
the history of his people,

of their exile, enslavement, wandering,
their law, the covenant of sharkskin

carried across the desert

Now, in our
historical epoch,

rat scat is precious,

is what is left of

revelation

       *

And then morning, after the night of the tooth fairy

the boy thinking of nothing
but what that small sum could buy

The mall, inconsolably distant

(No chance to shop

It was only Tuesday!)

This money, under the pillow,
useless, until the weekend,

brought a second loss more
painful than the first:

the days lost waiting

              till Saturday

The boy felt
wounded anew

       *

Another night, these updates on the bloodshed

these upticks in the death toll,
the footage, the smoke,

the blast-pattern,

the metal shreds

       *

Another night, lights go on and off

There seem to be lightning strikes across the street

       *

Another night, this could in the end be Antarctica

At the apex of the blue dome of the sky
the sun makes small circles

nothing but whiteness,
in one direction

in the other, a violet tinge

(This must be perfect freedom)

It's thirty below

I have left the vehicle
It's summertime

I'm in ecstasy

Wind shapes the snow

        *

           (It takes a certain disposition to

           live here. The depressed

           get choppered out)

        *

Another night, there is only one gun on Antarctica
They keep it in pieces

Keep the pieces in different places
           a disincentive to rash acts

on a continent no one

cares much about

Though long ago,

the Nazis staked a claim,
flying over vast tracts,

dropping swastika medallions on the snow

*

Our family greenhouses were at the end of the peninsula

the only part of Korea
not ravaged by

the Japanese

*

Bubbles in the ice crust at the edge of

a frozen creek where

a sandy beach appears in

the heart of a forest

*

The travelers, siblings,
don't like each other

They bicker on the way to the reading of
a will upon which what hope they have depends

*

Another night, the beasts bed down in the straw
          even the Alpine goats, so at home in the cold

*

And then morning, in archeological gravel,

          an ancient earring was found by its glint

*

(Loop your hair back
behind your ear

Pretend you are a primordial girl

Now look out at the prehistoric world,

　　its abundant resources
　　　　　　and scant population)

*

At a recent dinner party

the hostess looked old

Yet the meanness of a joke made present

what might yet be said, what

might be uttered

with a blush

*

Were the windows not black

　　trees would sweep down the hill to the brook

*

On the yellow lines of a road

that no one – thankfully —-
ever drives down

a man kneels
in the empty street

bows and presses his forehead

to the cement and tar

because, he says,
a great river once
ran beneath

*

Notes fly up from the
messianic clatter

*

The clarinet asks:
Will this then be the all of this that flows
from all of that?

*

As if there were a more to be

senselessly sensed

*

Reborn as we were said to be, and
knowing, presumably, the immensity of
what is not

*

The most encompassing of accounts reached
its furthest grasp

The infinite blew back through

hollowing out our vowels
like how wind rips open

the Badlands

*

Flakes light upon the feathers of birds
as they flutter and peck, melting,

in this one instance,

from the heat of the beating heart of
a bird the color of a snake

in Ecuador
notable for a poison

that de-coagulates the blood

*

Another night, one body lies down
and dies, another, arises

*

I have a ring for each finger on my left hand

I like nothing better now than to wave my hand in fresh sunlight
sideways like the tail of a fish resisting a current

*

The rain on the skylight turns crystalline in the cold

What cloud did the planet pass through last night?

*

Another night, be careful on the ice

As if, in the midst of an insurrection, you had

set fire to a palace and were fleeing across a frozen river

*

They say the best place to drop dead is a Las Vegas casino

Security cameras are everywhere

The staff sees you die, and revives you

*

You, as you so often are, with an empty vessel in each hand:
a champagne glass, and a brandy snifter

*

While you were out of the room

your philosophical epoch passed away

*

The concept of "experience"
is now an error

*

Another night, at this very table,

a beautiful woman once
                told truths

        She has chopped off her hair

                and now speaks to no one

    *

Another night, on a ridge in Chiapas

            The couple were high up, and very high . . .

                    On a boom-box, *Spiritual Unity*

    *

And then morning, police step back,

the paramilitaries cut loose

    *

The bay brightens. Afternoon light pouring over
clay-colored stones and raw earth

*

Snakes crawl from sewers to warm themselves on the pavement
(Taken, by some, to foretell prosperity)

*

A last beam of starlight warms one who

renounces sexual joy

who will die

naked at night

on a mountain of coal

*

Brick steps rise up in a field where
once stood an ancestral house

The steps stop at
a slab between
two cement guard dogs

which, with twilight,
bring to the violet air

Egyptian
intimations

*

Another night, on the far side of the horizon line,

the soul is an ascetic, so thin
she is shunned

*

(May mist bathe her skin,
her legs, her arms, her face

May her hair glisten from a light rain
and the air shine as she speaks)

*

As for me, all I have ever wanted to do is to bake cakes

And so I took a class, then two more,

one devoted solely

to decorating

Friends so loved my cakes
that soon I was making

everyone's
wedding cake

(It takes two days to make the layers

another whole day

for filling and frosting)

*

Another night, a communal garden,

seen from space, via satellite,
by a ballerina with a back problem

*

At sharp angles the ache stops
            I twist myself and continue

*

Beyond the trees a school bus breaks down

Its light dilutes in the white mist
along a road into a forest

A second bus appears

A line of children, barely visible,
file from one bus to the other

*

The thirst of the earth takes on a graceful insistence
like a stroke of cherry petal through the air

*

My hair is more ashen
than fire red now

*

Another night, in ancient Egypt,

        the soul says to the body:

        You are a tent made from a trash-bag

*

My house is owned by a set designer

No repairs are meant to last

What should be nailed
is merely stapled

*

Once a war hospital, our high school had photos

on the dining hall wall

Soldiers, savagely amputated,

are sitting out on a porch,
their solemn, stunned

faces as if asking,
"are we really alive?"

*

The true part of the soul is blank, and shines

the brightest when memories die

*

Foam stops at the shore but these moods

sweep me further

*

A leaf hangs sun-struck in space

A gossamer line holds it to the sky

A touch of air turns it silently

A leaf shot through with

light from all sides

     *

Some say a second mind lives

within the first and, now

     and then, breaks through

     *

Another night, the sky wants nothing more than to feel transformed
The sky calls all clouds into a fiery flow

     *

Here where no one

gets a job or moves away

Rather, all lives just well and dispel like

the shadow of a crucifix on the

wall of an abattoir

*

Another night, the paws of a dog splash in a pool

A storm tangles transmissions

A face shows itself to be suffering

    *

Orange, yellow, red, green, a tree all glowing all at once

like an icon into which the divine force floods

    *

Turmoil in a raindrop

As in that garage in Tacoma

      a former teacher started his car and slept

    *

Another night, chicken coops sweep out to sea
Hundreds of chickens, still squawking

    *

A refugee boat under dire conditions

each passenger vainly saving the last morsel of soap

still imagining a chance to freshen up

before a glorious land-fall

*

Another night, like a luminous spume on the sun,

like a vibrantly colored CD

dropped onto the wet runway of

a small, third world airport,

a CD with a drawing, in black,

of a tiger in a desert

*

Earlier bees gnawed out

the hole in the wall, to which

their offspring return

*

A dog bounds across the beach past a half buried iron wheel

with spokes of curved serpents

*

Stone portals look out now on water
          shining with light from the Arctic circle

*

Another night, in medieval Sweden,

the ghost of Henry James follows

the last thought to cross

into consciousness

at the moment of death

        *

                (He who made worlds for you to live in,

                   welcome him now in a place your mind has made)

      *

A beam from a lighthouse rakes the room at night
You feel like you are seeing a plane crash
from inside the cockpit

      *

Another night, next door, the pool party concludes

In the deadest hour, the last splashes and shrieks

They are young, next door   This may be

the great moment of their lives

      *

Paradise, a paroxysm,

     like a shunt that only

          momentarily fails

*

And then morning, I remain fearful about my rebirth

Already I see, as if through an amniotic sheen,

gold light shining through blood

*

I feel like hands are lifting me out of my own heart

*

The chorus was often held, by later playwrights, to be

archaic, extraneous, and cumbersome

Yet at various times in my life

I was called to be a member,

to interrogate, console, council,

exhort, and survive,

at times with open palms

pressed to the side of my face

mouth an O

eyes wide beside

a gate that had been left open

*

Another night, a balloon, tied to a keyboard, floated over the sea

Whatever makes birds raucous is happening right now

A cherished comfort is taken away

A kiss takes the dream in a new direction

No one draws near a dog so lost

If only a shadow could be seen before it falls

FOAM INTO FOAM

c

As When Icecaps Fall Back

(Such deliberations
as come to hospice nurses
when the dying object: no more
consults! No more
options! Don't show me
one more test result!
Show me only
a pyramid of
martini glasses,
and, beside it, a list of the
world's greatest gins)

*

dream

A world's edge, seen through heat,
through wavering bursts of purity rising
back towards the sun, from
this place, mountains
rising around, chalky stripes
sloping upward where the two,
(he having just exclaimed
"I don't know you at
all, so what can this
delirium mean?")
were about to fall in love,
heedlessly, and forever, her face
the outward form, in all
its beauty, of some
resolved tragedy,
turning towards him, away
from untrammeled stone
and glittering pools, the earth
having taken millennia of

poisons within itself,
and nullified their effect,
the earth being too
magnificent to abide
defilement. As if looking
at the earth, there, had ended
some pain for her, and now she
would kiss him, a kiss that,
in that place, seemed
contrary to all other kisses,
those where pleasure pours
in from the mouth, wells up behind
the eyes, dissolves all thought,
cascades down the throat,
bringing the body from
death to life. With *this* kiss,
long, intense, subtle in its pulse
and pace, the ecstasy
radiates from bones into
flesh and skin, drawn, at last,
to the mouth, a kiss so long, those
with them on this desert trek
gasped, seeing this kiss
as unlike any ever given
before, a kiss about
to begin some vast
transformation, of the
place, and of those in it,
as if the kiss was not the
crown of this mysterious
journey, but the cause,
so that all could feel a joy
none had any idea existed, rise
into each, as if from the earth itself

*

When mortals ascend, St Anselm said,
they join with those aspects of
the Godhead that are on the far
side of the perceptible, that
can barely be grasped by
the mind at all, so deeply
embedded in Paradise as
these souls now are
The sensation is not of
rising, but of falling, as
when icecaps fall back
into the sea, so we're free
to infer, now that kayaking
is allowed, in rivers once so
low they seem closed for repair
Expiation had long been of
no concern, yet it seems,
amid whirling snows, that
entering higher forms of
thought will require
a heart-felt expostulation
upon the seven sacred wounds

*

Lord, may even just one some-such wound

quietly ruin me

May I, finally, crawl up

onto the cross, hug

the suffering Christ,

and cry out to my

failing Lord:

"Through me, feel

what ray of light striking

your skin has travelled the farthest . . ."

WITHOUT RENT OR SEAM

Pushed to

    polish, urged

        to burnish . . .

      *

            (Instead,

            the interim staff at

            the library

            knocked the

            heads

            off the pedestals,

            and threw

            them

            down the

            elevator

            shaft)

WITHOUT RENT OR SEAM

Later in life, he just
sat home on the Sabbath,
setting off explosives in his back yard
until the cops showed up
"Though raised Catholic,"
he would say, "I never
got when to kiss the ring"
Finally, he slipped away,
as if down the river Thoreau
sailed, red, brown, peach,
copper, silver on the
tree-lined water, the flow
as garish as the fence around
the temple on the bluff
by the waterfalls, a
derelict estate bought
by a volcano cult
Believers wed on the
seething rim, birthed
their kids over fumes,
dropped their dead into
the pulsating interior
This, their last spiritual
home, found them sadly
distant from the geo-
thermal infernos that
were the truth of
their ritual life

Last Supper in a Red Desert

after a painting by M.F. Husain

The turning of thought is all,
like the shadow of a massive hawk
falling across the floor of a room
after a pitch-black night on a footbridge
the day Judas hung himself. The sun
reaches the top of my head
and Christ is harrowing hell
In a photo taken by aiming
a cheap flash camera at
a mirror in the dark, my face
floats above a liberation of light
All's calm, bright, falling from afar
Clouds of blossoms spot the earth
A girl recently said: when the devil
opens his book, with all the bad
you done written out, your
page will be unreadable,
drenched in the blood of Jesus
A banquet table has been set
in the desert. It is a gold band across
a red backdrop. The apostles are
crumpled gold foil next to a camel
Like Machado hearing Bergson,
Paris, 1910, I, too, concede
"There is something immortal
in us that wants to die with
whatever dies." In the dimness of
closing rain the letter is hard to read
The return address is a glacier
in Greenland where a loss
touches many lives at once
I was speaking to my father

then I woke up. A bird was
exceptionally exuberant,
then day turned into a dark
white flowered branch beneath
a smear of grey. I am sorry
I have hidden you away,
my sister, but your feelings
are so joyful they would earn
scorn and envy on this bitter earth
But I, too, believe the light is
called out of the earth by music
As for today, my plan is to dispel
whatever keeps me apart from
perfection, even as a face
never seen directly is
about to show itself. Were
this desolation the Dome of
the Rock, Love would descend,
saying: Look: I have broken
all of this open, for you

The Gates of Alexandria

We were free at night to give away
jewels, carvings, rare stones,
until no possession was
left except the glow of a face
and, yes, in those days, were
people worth deriding
No point now in poking fun
The powerful and otherwise
famous have lives so
fantastic or disastrous
it's humiliating to
even mention them
As for us, we dwindle like
a named tropical storm that
turns away from land
We damage nothing
We fall back into
"disorganized elements"
until some future brushwork
puts a mad pulse in the
colors, in the planet
the paint creates
A couple lie on a bed
in a house by the sea
She's telling him what
it's like to be a prosecutor
in Northern California
They may be about to kiss,
then one or the other mingles
with the sound of surf
The light is interleaving
streaks of violet
over the ocean and
the weekend drifts away,

untended. The life we left is
now illumined only by
our absence from it
We bend, meld, waver,
disperse, search, ascend,
disseminate, migrate, begin,
in the annihilation and
rebirth of all circumstance,
to do favors for a double
gone west, who made
a movie discarded
by a local library where
you work night shift
at the information desk
Your coworker, a lesbian
with a birth defect, is, for you,
the only love that matters
During the day you gather up
any ribald memory she
might find amusing
in the long hours
commencing as soon
as you swing on your
crutches through the door
you call the gates of Alexandria,
your city, the true and
only end of your thought,
where life is desire, where
Antony dreads his doom,
Caesar, whose oars beat
the sea to opal, and
Cleopatra cries
out: "Hand me that
basket of serpents!
I will not endure
the indignity of a
pleasure that is ending"

CAPE VERDE

Sometimes I think
horses are immortal,
and that I live
in a barn on
Mt. Olympus,
that my body is
pure mind, and minds
are dreams whirling
within a derelict
infinity: Last night,
for example,
I had sex with
a powerful partner
I, too, was neither
man nor woman
Under the billowy
satin we both
explored our
mutual dearth
of genitalia
I awoke as
happy as after
a great ravishment

Cape Verde II

Once, there was a delicious
cake in the shape of
a book. I ate
a chapter
When I finished,
my daughter was
grown up and
gone
I was in the
Cape Verde Islands
Rain-shine, sunlit leaves
There on my own, to
scope out
the most ghostly
of housing
projects,
feeling,
amid such
mimosa, unreal

The Protestant Conscience

for Mark Scroggins

Midmorning moon, seas,
peaks, and craters overhead
Heavenward, the spiral of tree sap
An x-ray astounds a doctor
who says, "No skeleton
is scant of grandeur." Days,
nothing to do. But night is
still a temple to be led through
The day feels un-bandaged
Does the sun have a wick?
Does the world wobble?
Only from a screen in the
dark can others so touch me
(I feel wet, empty, shining,
unready for life.) The map
has a beautiful finish, faint
waves of blue blow through it,
then a braid of grey shapes
where the words whirl away
amid monsters and imperiled
souls. In a recent surgical respite
they dug out my face and
sent me home with fluid
to pour through a tube into
my new hollow, like a
spring bubbling all silver
in a bone grotto. I am purified,
pledged anew to embracing
the miraculous burble of
the cure flowing into me
I am a wounded knight beside
a healing niche in a forest

A beautiful sprite leans close,
confides: "My hot flashes
are finally over. Nature's so
done with me. The leaves
have my permission to turn
their colors, the torrent to
seep into the brick"

WITHOUT RENT OR SEAM

A heap of cinderblock at
sunset. The derelict mall is
now other than what thought
can bring about. Soon, this
dusty basement will be
the primordial canopy
where the last birds alight
Soon, universal forces
will concentrate in Jane,
seen, by chance, on local TV,
an inadvertent extra, on
the street, as beautiful
now as, years back, at her
wedding, when the
water rose over the pier,
then dropped so low that
by evening the river
had disappeared

THE GREATER ADVENTURE

You, however,
are handed a ribbon
for a race you did not
run while others
lie about, suffering
from gunshot wounds
Not many triumph
over time, though
a wayward derelict,
a Stephano like
yourself, can
have a brother
who never left home,
who finds passing from
room to room the
greater adventure
He is content
to be just there,
even as a cold blue
dioxide light falls on
your seemingly
ghastly days

Periphery Dance Hall

for Simon Pettet

The proximity of a planetary pole

can be felt inside luxurious

hotels in any

number of Nordic lands

I'm here for the holiday pageant at the firehouse
at the edge of town on an expanse that could be called a prairie

but for craters and ice floes

The parking lot is empty
A white bird flies out of black smoke

That chunk of grey ice is the sky

Pinwheels of light

slowly turning   inside a head

Social integration

seems easier here yet

never has anyone known you less well

How silently the rain came and went in the night

This is what is, for now, for you,

the beyond:

        a sky falling into the street

Yesterday, a hint hurt me
an intimation left me perplexed

Dropping the camera again might just fix it

(The blur makes us all seem energetic,
about to abandon our bodies)

In this hotel, discredited ideas

cleansed of apparent purpose

are highly prized

And nothing can break
the new lock on the door

Shoot it with a gun, it won't open

any intruder will have to split the door open with an axe

The run-off seems to weave itself

The lip of a waterfall shines above the black

In an 1825 painting by John Martin

Sadak is looking for

a sip of oblivion

But winter is the well all fall into

Torch bearing children singing on a hillside
A flock of belled goats is released

Such joy, as if your brothers and your sister
are talking in the next room

Snow streaks the forest floor

(Let a wounded face be the final icon)

Last night you were inside a mobile home
speeding down a highway

It was dark and quiet

The bed had fresh linen on it

You were anticipating

a restful sleep

though there was also this
sensation of shooting through space

It felt precarious

An intermittent sideways wind
made the room waver

WITHOUT RENT OR SEAM

Let other revelations dye the sky
of those who hide among us
like music store clerks
murmuring about
new kinds of music
Sadly, there's no time
to catch a recommendation
You forgot to load up
the furniture that is
your destiny to
deliver, in a rental
van, to a roofless ruin
with floors of wet moonlight

Without Rent or Seam

Little of your day to day
is enviable, yet you prefer
not to die only seeing the
hell of it all, only glorying
in the many mirrors of
your own mayhem
A dead stag with white
granite chips for eyes
seems about speak
with a warmth often
denied the un-addicted
But then, an envelope,
full of the ashes of other
envelopes, is in your hand
You put it down, just a second,
and now it has mingled
with shadows and
can't be found

Done Then, Gasped at Now

A bright peak floats in mid air
A mountain that seems like a tree
grown parallel to the ground,
reaching toward sunlight
from the depth of shade
We have yet to become dust
on the road to the court of God
but peace comes while looking
over the water. A house is
wrapped in white plastic
Low voices, sounds of tools
Weeks of mild wonder at the
jeweled tower that is gathering
within the veil, the temple of
Solomon, restored at last
Thought rides on waves to
far places. Early sun fills the
stream of water in the air
The girl down the block will be
sent off to a tough love camp
The son of the judge will turn up
at a Salvation Army barrack
Before the tabernacle is opened
we will become birds of the Spirit
Amid the Chinese food cartons
the crows are a surly choir
I heard a woman say hello
in a far room, no one was there
The movie last night? Terrible
The actors seemed ashamed
They seemed to be saying,
between their dismal lines,
forget you saw this

*

Semen shines in the dark of
a glistening rain-washed street
where the stones are brightening
beneath the heels of apocalyptic
survivalists running wild past
a black dog with a red aura
A girl lies on a lawn, a yellow
flower resting on her belly
like a whirlwind of doves white
and grey sweeping a famous sea
that seethes like shadows of leaves
But now, a fish in the claws of
a heron makes a promise: pain
will prove a purpose beyond itself
Then a cake is placed on the table
(The spirit of the age was elsewhere)
Nonetheless, you have understood
nothing: not a turnip, a potato
a yucca root, an icon saved
from the flood, or an earth
struck by asteroids more often
than admitted. No one here
handles the paint well, daubs
festoon the room we were hired
to turn white. But this is how
homes are made, lives lived
within them, until we awaken
elsewhere, rain beating the roof,
like a woman saying: Can't you help me
get over this? Nothing can be done
beyond the gentle pulse of
lightning pops by which I
slosh this down. Barely time,
in a life, to intuit the warring of

earth and sky, as set forth in
The Oresteia, by torchlight, on
the mountaintops at night

*

Treated well and yet unhappy,
wandering down a corridor, white
pillars lead to a small, black door
Here and there angels whisper
A dove crests the air above the shed
A faint gold light on the scene
A haphazard transfiguration
We slept on the ferry and awoke
entering the port of an astonishing city
A medical panic had me on the phone
The consulate broke protocol and got us
into a first-rate clinic, with doctors
who went to school in England
But, when we left, they didn't even
bother to pull out the IV needle
Dank halls of bloodied locals
This must be the gospel where demons
are driven into pigs, pigs are driven
over a cliff and into the sea
This must be the gospel where
the Redeemer gets secretive,
casts us into bewilderment,
the gospel where redemption is
a telescope in orbit around Venus
picking up the heat signature of
any rock speeding in from the beyond
But who could believe such fruit
finds its way into a sherbet?
This is the oldest landmass
in the world, he said. This ground

is more soaked in blood than
any other dirt on earth. But
the river is shallow and sandy
Warm, clear, you can swim in it
Dolphins come right up to the dock,
ready for Messianic time to start
Until then, the rabbi said, this world
belongs to Batman and The Joker

*

Wall Street is largely underwater
A dog slinks along the high ground
A man without a shirt has clearly
had significant chest surgery
He waits for word to arrive
from the cave in the sky time
goes back to when it's done
I am gracious, but out of sync
On a mountainside in some land
yet to be called holy three flare forth
None there to witness and adore
Instead, you're walking along the icy wall
your mother walked on top of, once,
in summer, with her sister, both
still girls, off to visit a friend
Here's the big wide porch of
the house they grew up in
She talked about it all the time
You heard about every room inside
It belongs to someone else now
You will never see the inside
of that house, never see
your mother again. The lawn
drops to a ditch, a perfect place
to lie down and cry. In your

long winter coat, you do that
The sun warms your face, as if
you had found the last
possible paradise

OUTCRY AT TWILIGHT

Otherwise, this would be the hour

the lovers drink poison

        *

Resplendent One, revive them

        *

So that, years later, by
              chance, each will die

again, and at the

         same moment

(But truly, this time, and apart, direly

wed to parodies
            of each other)

        *

         So, bereft
         and abed, in the
         longest night's ever
         darkening purple,
         I reason,
         as if I had
         never felt, on that
         snow-blown veranda,
         the first tremble of all reckonings

*

And the snow on the ground,
Beneficent One, you brightened only
enough, at last light,
on winter
solstice, that
the pit of each
raindrop
welled with
intriguing shadow

*

(As if, in the beyond, a beautiful woman
in a black cloak has long
loved you in secret
and, now that
you're dead,
she will
introduce
herself, and tell you
about her
passion)

FOAM INTO FOAM

A touch of wonder is now
welcome on all levels of being

Dawn is impressive

But so are the nights that
occur inside the sun

＊

The two cousins ran down onto the beach at night,

stood in the surf to hide

the sound of the can as it opened
Bubbles breaking on lips

a harsh soda, prickly
waves fell around them

The sound of the sea hid them

Terrible taste, that beer, dumped out,

foam to foam. Bury the
can in wet sand

＊

Snow brightening the shadows

of the branches

*

Night a fateful letter just dropped in the mailed

Days, few, before it arrives

A letter the sun sends the earth

written in fire, as if to say:

What could be done, has been

*

Nights of bones boiling all night
Roots, greens, spices, meat

Scraps from the feast

A hint of extinction

a guess at revelation

Pilgrims along the road
Begging bowls

Steam rising from
a ladle or a spoon

*

The emissaries have all fled

No one wanted to say such words

*

Demeter is in deep despair

*

Such nights as snow falls in celebration
of the ineradicable warmth
consciousness
is about to reclaim

*

Such nights as might be spoken of in an apocryphal gospel

The apostles ask Mary how she came to

conceive the incomprehensible

How, that is, they said,

she could carry within her what

cannot be carried

"Lord, the seven heavens could
hardly contain Thee yet

Thou was pleased to be
contained in me . . ."

So with a prayer
she began but before
the answer

fire shot from her mouth

Soon all Creation
was aflame, burning

to the point of
annihilation. Finally

amid unbearable

combustion

Jesus was again in their midst
and said to his mother:

"Say no more, or all this
will come to an end"

        *

On a motel balcony, at twilight

Alligators scuttle into a swimming pool

A rising wind blows away the sun

        *

Imperfection must thrive in you
Consider your impulse

to reenact, in the realm of
the interpersonal, what
your ancestors once

did to villages

There's an aura about you
of smoke and blood

The carnage of your charm
ignites the entire office

But outrages are
overlooked because
you are such fun to be with

*

Yes, a yen for pain, but now pain has
turned pure, like an autumn
tree finally free
of its leaves

*

True, no one has died but
a new life can be discerned

As in the glowing depth of
an obsidian mirror where

gods of death are looking out
at notable contemporary artworks

*

A composer writes a number on a blackboard
He draws an axis, then another, then
a third, the third curves, the
diagram gets too dense to follow
this depth of musicality
abides beyond you

until, should it happen,
all notes are struck,
and a drumbeat levitates
the room as, head in hands,
rocking, nodding, you,
there in the front row,
start, as is said,
"losing your shit"
as the other instruments
kick in, the bass, the piano
Little is left of you, or the night
as once known by you

*

That rape, in a forest, in autumn
The night the leaves let go all at once

*

Having dismissed all hint

of a higher life

yet eaten the seeds:

ruby-colored, dark blueish core

*

The goddess, your mother, finds you

Her hair falls across

your eyes as

she consoles you:

141

*

"Not ever what once was, but more

than the

nothing of now"

THE DISAPPEARANCE OF FATE

When ever God fills me with his fullness
I shall see the disappearance of fate.
— Emerson

The earth, the sky,
the ashes in the sparkle
that will be a beach
A stone there
has a reddish spot
in the rounded
grey-white that
opens me to infinity
—- as in this crazy math
proving the upper
and lower ends
of a cone are
the same. I
am, at the same time,
on the ground,
and in the
plane coming
towards me
through
the clouds

*

No light
of beyond
will be lying
within the coming
dark, as some
infinities
lie within

others
like a brick
lies in a very
old wall,
in sunlight,
red, rust,
orange
with
smears
of charcoal

*

As when one in

chronic pain says:

Who I am is

not how I feel

*

Who I am is

silver and mercury
in a bath of nitric acid

is a glittering spider,
a "tree of Diana"

Who I am is

iron dropped in
hydrochloric acid, boiled
to dryness, then a powdery

silicate mix of sand
and potassium
carbonate gets
mixed in

Who I am is

a kind of garden
in which the ruddy
ferric chloride
bifurcates, rises,
reaching towards
the sunlight,
bursting into
root-like
veins of metal
found by miners
deep in the earth,
like twinned
ores of
silver
and gold,
growing under-
ground, reaching
up, ripening

*

Who I am
rises in answer
to the sun, though
exhaustion is all the
sun really feels, a million
times more than we do,
yet the sun returns,
it stays awake

every morning
as molecules meld
atop a Mayan pyramid
where kneel adepts of
a Toltec master
Each scoops
from the dirt
around the ruin
a hand-sized
grave, burying
the evil self each has
cast into a pebble
chosen for its likeness
to the black sun feeding the white
sun from within
Whereas here,
slack bamboo pods
treasure, through
the day, the tint of
deepest blue
night pours into
them, love's
very flood

*

So that morning's
calm may be enlivened by
multiple hurricanes
erupting hundreds
of miles south,
over the waters
As if suffering
might lift me out of
disunity and distance
while sunflowers compose

a wreath dropped
from a boat,
a mother's ashes
poured through
the drifting
ring, into
"an unknown
mode of being"

*

The sun places a low island
of light on the horizon,
another of stone
beside it, and
before both,
a glittering path,
alive only a short while
as the sun lifts higher,
a straight way,
through water, earth,
and the thought of darkness

*

Burnished water

Sky overcast and silver

Surfers idle and look back
towards the horizon,

now and then
catch a wave

pulling up

just before
the Golgotha
of rocks

*

At the tide-line
well-dressed girls

take pictures of
each other

*

Those there
for the memorial

climb over the

guardrail

and plod onto the beach

*

No more tributes, salutes, no more
honoring the meander
of a life. Now, the
frothy disposal
A hurricane closing,
sea too rough for a boat
The man, his mother's ashes
in a bag, in hand, steps
slowly over rocks
Rush of water, twist

of foam wherever
he steps or staggers
He is entering
the endlessness
his mother adored, looked out on
from her boarding house,
that last scrap of
the 19th century
on this strip of coast
Wife, daughters, back at
water's limit
Grievous progress
Half soaked, he stakes
himself against a rock,
looking a long time
out at the waves
He glances back to
shore, red with emotion
Hot tears drop into the sea
Primordial dust in
his hands, that which
was made, which
then made him
Continent's drop
Surfers sit idle
A churn, a glide
Gulls look on as the
dust forsakes
the name it had,
is released, free of
joy, of grief, of
all memory. The
dust swirls from
the bag. He pours it,
the grieving man, heir
of a fallen house

Grit blows against rock
He dips down at last,
gently rinses out
the plastic bag
Sea-swollen clarity
The last of the ashes
tint the glitter, a
creature once rife
with passion, anger,
generosity, love
and her share of the
highs and lows of fortune
All is at an end. All
returns to the long
tapering curls of the sea
All lives pass between
immense swells
All alive sense where
in the tide they occur,
whether pulled to,
or away from, shore,
and the immense depth
upon which the surfers perch,
ready to ride what the
storm sends this way
The man trundles
to shore, folds the bag
He slips it in a drenched
pocket, and says: "It is
what it is. That's all
I can say to you
It is what it is"

*

The oldest of
the three on the
dimly lit
street
climbs
in a taxi to
his hotel. The
youngest
heads up a hill
on foot to his
dorm. Chilly
evening
The man
between the
two, son of
one, father of
the other,
says
bye
to both

*

On the river, seven red boats
The water is choppy and bright
The boats are sailboats
On each sail, a word. The
boats wind in and out
of each other. They
form smaller groups
against the city skyline
Some sails are turned away
And, as the words are
only on one side of
each sail, at any time
on this fall afternoon,

to one by the water, to one
watching the weaving of
the boats, only some
of all of the words
can be read: Never
Forget. We Never
Forget. (Note. This is
not holocaust art, but
Lockheed Martin's motto)

WE NEVER FORGET WHO

WE'RE WORKING FOR

        *

     (From another spot on the water
     the boats boast: We're Never
     Working. Or, Forget Working
     Or, Forget Who For)

    *

So adoration tips toward
bright, beautiful
gods who ruin
all while liberating
the wind, which I drink in
like a champagne
with cognac, bitters,
and sugar, until
the lid of
thought opens
like a portable altar from
Mexico: tiny statues,
candles, and a

village made of
clay bricks
A man there
hefts hay up a hill
led by a bird
come to earth
to break in two the
presumed inviolability
of cause and effect,
that insufferable
shackle that
keep me here,
craving an access
of lucidity not otherwise
due until death, that
last Halloween
no kids come
to the door,
not even to the
cool fire of foils left
in a bowl on the top step

*

What survived of
the composer's atonal
score resembled a rise
in a run of gullies,
the slope and sweep
of them fading
into a desert while
the ridges of shadow
betray the sun
passing over
a marvelous city,
a new home, should

truth arise from a recent
witless insult
and burn down
the dungeon where
the lost lie, where you
note a red bird, maybe
a cardinal, running
up, down, beat-up
porch boards

*

Or, maybe, eternity will return
more the way rain wicks
through chimney
brick: The red
dampens, then
darkens

Absynthe Cake

Birds sleep during the day
My mind is almost as
small as theirs, so when
I say I have a lot on my
mind it's more like
a kind of singing,
a vanishing point
not on the canvas
but within the viewer,
like a glacier that washes
over a mountain, shimmering
pine needles rolling
over chunks of ice
that slide down,
becoming a stream
where, in the distance,
an icon is held up to a blaze
A village flashes into ash
Finally, in despair, a priest
flings the icon into
the intensifying fire
"Well if you won't help us,
see if you can help yourself!"
I woke to find my room
full of chains, and
the tennis court flooded
Everyone lies, but the lie shines
with its own glorious truth,
a pillar of flame before
which Brahma
becomes a goose,
flies up, but cannot find
the crest of the roaring
Then Vishnu, a boar,

digs into the earth
for a 1000 years yet
cannot find the
lower limit of
the conflagration
Then the flame opens
Siva, inside the niche
of incandescence
reveals himself as
the lord of all,
and prophesies:
"This life is like
a present from the
madhouse gift shop,
a contortion of wire
piercing the heart of a candle,
the wick, inexplicably,
juts from its side
The mangle of
script on the card
seems to say:
Not to be burned
till the end of
the world,
till the morning
a bird is only
incidental to its song
the notes happening by
at the moment
a throat was needed"
Then came a joyous yelping from
the kennel at the end of
the street as day rises
into the sky
over the Japanese
fountain on the

former slave
plantation where,
when a girl, all gathered
on my birthday for
absinthe cake
This was back when
my father still made an
effort to translate into English
so I could feel I was
a part of what
was said. But now
that we're back in Poland
he doesn't do that
He doesn't want to
be my father anymore
He just wants to be
in the world in
some older way
It made sense,
but it startled me,
that our roles in life
are only that, and
that they end

WITHOUT RENT OR SEAM

Noon feels like night

The fragrance of tobacco bales
intoxicate a non-smoker

Each soul gets a chance to
not accept Creation

A lake breaks across a dock

Dizzied by beauty I cut my hand

A nerve disturbance

causes those who live
in the blue hills

to see them as red

The last of the green yellowing
in the crease of the last leaf

A marsh aflame
at sunset,

a black boat

At the bakery, a girl

on tiptoes,

on her bare thigh
a bruise, or a lick of

bicycle grease

THE SECRET HISTORY OF SECRETS

You would like to feel
a dreaming mind makes
all this. And, you're part of it,
you are a dream, and shot
through with deep joy,
knowing that all you see,
hear, taste, touch and smell
passes through you, floods
the greater mind, that
dreams all, a mind
curious about all that is,
each moment, coming to be
As if this were the first time
the world could be truly
seen, a stream flowing
both ways at once, though
appearing so still, none
could say for sure
it moved at all. Perhaps
all is always rushing
the same way, at the
same rate: rocks, sand,
banks, trees on the banks,
the days, months, years
All is cascading, taking up
and dropping forms,
the way a favorite actress
goes from role to role. Once
she was a fighter pilot
in a space opera
Later, a detective
amid a murder spree
But you remember how,
stranded on a planet, once,

she looked up lost into
the deep of sky

*

Touch each of your open eyes
with a forefinger. Now, feel
a breeze sweeping across
a glacier. Afterwards,
see what you've been
awaiting your whole life:
an upside down Nativity!
Trees, root-end up, from
rafters. Bodies weave
through the tops. Gongs
ring. A weird music wells
from beyond a sheet
The smell of the pine
is delightful and eerie and
in tribute to whoever lay
beneath the last pine lid
sanded smooth in this
gutted garage, once
a coffin factory, now
a dangling, Cabbalistic
wilderness. Each branch
is a stage in the arc of
divine energy pouring
down in deep seeps
into this art-space
where a woman's voice
elaborates a single syllable
that wraps around and
through the trees

*

Even more, a film is playing:
yellow stripes disappear
under the front of the
questing car. Headlights
flash across briars. Visible
in a spit of winter grass,
a wind exalts our spirits
Branches bend over
the stones in a stream
Amid clouds, drifting
leaves, shadow of the
one filming, alive in
the flow, as if we're all
a split second ahead of
our own thought, so that
the past is right "here,"
in ripples of return

*

A corral, a man walks the horse
towards you. You've never
seen a real horse. The man
says, the horse is small
and gentle. To you,
he is huge and fiery
The horse snorts smoke
You reach up, touch
the bristle. Skin quivers
The sun has just come up
You can feel the horse
seeing you. Then,
your father catches
you under each arm and
sets you in the saddle
The plunge of the hoofs

rises up through you
The dawn is chilly
Your wonder keeps
your blood rushing
Warmth flows into you,
from the sun, and from
the great beast that bears you
You float in fear and delight
The head dips, grazes
In the stillness, the fields
rush, out and away

*

Maybe a novel will come in the mail,
a good read, a small pleasure,
a modest sublimity that has
moved many more
than once, that holds
a truth only shown those
who suffer to such a degree:
those whose mania will
not let them sleep, whose
anxieties keep them
apart, constantly sick
from medication, words
to distract that man from the dark
roadside abyss he stands by

*

The day has been delayed
That great surge of light is
falling, must be, on some
other planet today, on
craters of ice or lava

or gravel from meteors,
on all that lifeless matter
that spins around the earth,
whatever turns around
us as we turn around
in what are, presumably,
our resurrection bodies

      *

(More likely, we are, each of us,
alone in a room, blindfolded,
headphones full of white noise,
heads picking up images sent
a considerable distance by
someone concentrating
on a picture, scientifically
proving us gifted "receivers"

Now I am seeing a hotel in Vienna

I see an emerald-colored hot tub

The whirls look heavenly

Those in the hot tub say

"A child has been born. His
name is something like Sigil")

      *

There's no real way,
an authority assures me,
to find an event in time
or in space. There is only

before, after, only here,
there. Only a point when,
wide awake, it's like you
come home many years
gone and find, to your joy,
the old kinship system
had kept a niche for you,
like that tangle of branches
that is a horizon with light
flying across it, towards
a kind of defeat rarely
heard of, because it is
followed by delight

*

It could be: to follow
is to foretell, is to bring
back what has never yet been
Understanding is now open,
is now pried wide, by
an interrelated run of
thoughts that might
otherwise compose
an experimental film
which takes as its theme
the denial of life, real life,
the life about which you've
never written, regarding
which are no witnesses,
concerning which, no
direct utterance has
ever been made, from
which no sensation
arises, about which,
all memories mislead,

the life behind or within
or around what is said to be
known, the life that renders
the empirical unreal, that
proves the baseless is
the fount of all

*

You have touched the sun
and found it to be cool. You
took it down from the sky
The light hung there. On
a winter field, you spread
the sun before you like it was
no more than a ground-cloth of
celestial origin. And you
lay on it, felt warmth from
within the winter earth itself
Without closing your eyes
you began dreaming

JOSEPH DONAHUE's books include *Before Creation*, *World Well Broken*, *Incidental Eclipse*, *Red Flash on a Black Field*, *Wind Maps I-VII*, and the ongoing multi-volume poem, *Terra Lucida*, comprised of *Terra Lucida*, *Dissolves*, and *Dark Church*. He also co-edited *Primary Trouble: An Anthology of Contemporary American Poetry* and *The World in Time and Space: Towards a History of Innovative Poetry in Our Time*. He is the co-translator of *First Mountain*, along with its author, Zhang Er.

Made in the USA
Columbia, SC
02 March 2020